Secrets of Elevation

Hidden in

Stirring Poems

Secrets of Elevation

Hidden in

Stirring Poems

Dr. Udo F. Ufomadu

C & P
Ufomadu Consulting & Publishing

Published by:

Ufomadu Consulting & Publishing

P.O. Box 746

Selma, AL 36702-0746

www.UfomaduConsulting.com

ISBN 0-9754197-6-5
Library of Congress Catalog Card Number: 2005901728

Acknowledgements

Special thanks to my parents Ezekiel Ufomadu and Evelyn Ufomadu for the seed they planted in me. Thanks also to all cherished friends and family members who prayed and supported me.

Contents

Contents

Contents

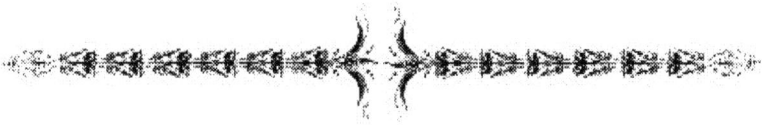

Faith Without Works

Swim with me through this river of hope,
Together we'll arrive at the beautiful shore of sanguinity.
Our faith we understand a lot,
Our prayer we utilize over and above,
But our action is now and then tormented to stagnancy.
As our visions and good thoughts come and go
With no action,
So do our opportunities appear and disappear.
When we stack and pile our visions
With no action
So unpleasant does such reflection manifests
On our promise.
It is disgusting,
When dreams are destroyed
By fear of mortal disapproval.
It is not beauteous
When faith stands alone
Without works.
It is unbiblical to say, "I love you"
Without showing love through
prayer, support, & sharing.
It is even an abomination
When good people diminish for lack of exploits,
For that person who avoids praying,
Also avoids the energy source.
For that person who avoids planning,
Also avoids a map to an expected destination.
For that person who avoids making mistakes,
Also avoids growing up in life spiritually,
materially, & physically.
For that good individual who has not grown lately,
Has not tried something new lately.

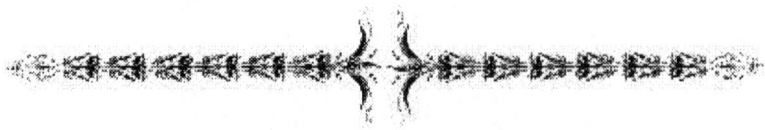

Praise Offering

Praising you Lord ignites my fire
With good melody, good people, I will not tire
Accept this offering that I hold so dear
And shower me that love that holds me near

I fell into an explosion of divine favor
I'm devoured in the flood of this love
It's not like I never envisioned
But never did I envisage my heart so magnetized

Now play me a tranquil melody of hope
That my faith may explore
Play me that serene tune of praise, I beg
That my soul may flourish and bless my Lord.

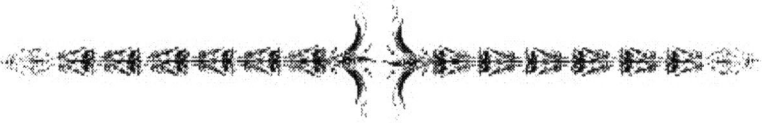

Inspiration

*I hold fast as my compass, the instructions of a heavenly
father:*

When the plan has not materialized,
HOPE
When materialization takes longer than man expects,
COPE
When the devil whispers a lie,
NOPE

Let's fetch from the prosperity stream that flows steadily:

When the prophecy bell rings of your soul's prosperity,
BELIEVE
When the entire stream is ordered to overflow,
RECEIVE
When heaven sends a perfect container,
RELIEF

I found refuge in a Supernatural that changes not:

When your friends act like adversaries,
PRAY & GUARD
When an innocent child spits on devil's face,
PRAISE & APPLAUD
When all God's children have one enemy,
PROGRESS & UPWARD

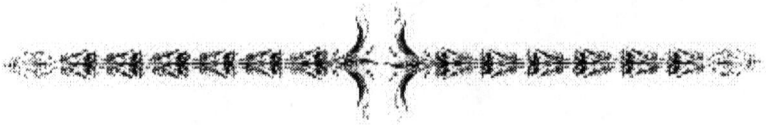

Exclude the Unwanted

To God be all the glory
For His grace manifested a story
For His mercy will manifest your story
As you tread to everlasting glory

To an expensive liquor
Has a hand reached out to kill
A liver so needed;
Being unfair to a gift

To a tobacco company
Was a seed sent to
Deteriorate a lung so needed;
Being unfair to a gift

To God's work and to love
Has a seed reached out to,
Helping self, helping others;
Being fair to gifts and harvests.

To God be all glory
His grace manifested a story
His mercy will manifest your story
As you tread to everlasting glory.

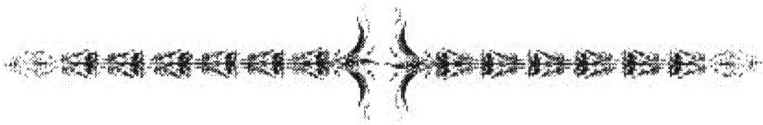

Best is Yet to Come

Neatly stacked, secured by God,
Is your very best.
Initial bold attempt
Passed a crucial test,
Engineering the shatter of all devil's blocks,
Blocks fashioned to intimidate your best.

Your faith has worked out a pride,
As indecision was utterly disgraced,
Even procrastination and frustration were defied
When prayer conquered, when prayer displaced obstacles,
While abomination was hostaged and tied.
Your good trampled as your better replaced.

The preamble of a move is what we've seen,
Your best is packed for a surprise.
The devil's obstructive machine
Will never deter a success of divine price.
Your faith in God, your belief in forgiveness, have cleaned
All negative buildups, giving way for prosperity to suffice.

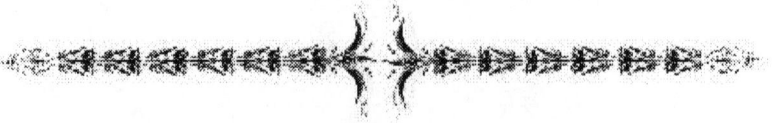

Order My Footsteps, Lord

Very much like any good planner
Positive thoughts bound together
Good seeds proliferate here and there
First class grounds connected far and near
In every instance my soul cries
Order my footsteps, Lord

An average guitar player of course
My strings tuned right this season
Happiness for my God and me
Smile on faces around me
And a prayer must still say
Order my footsteps, Lord

Felt in the vein of a great ball player
The penetration pass was just right
Anxiety and hope overwhelm him
His score, their joy
Yet a plea must utter
Order my footsteps, Lord

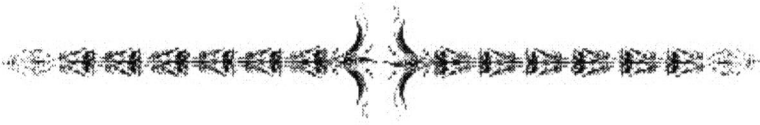

Control

I have defined my own self
And my faith- armor- revealed itself
When mortals attempted to place and stigmatize
While devil endeavored to grade and criticize

The heights and goals did wisdom request
Mastery of associations with others did knowledge demand
And a good relationship with God did understanding
request
Even my Plan for the future did wisdom request

We thought of a better day
But faith and works secured a pay
On peace did we meditate day and night
On solid ground did we stand rain or shine

A desire to prosper spiritually
Even the longing to flourish materially
And a move to become all that I wanted to become
Did I conceptualized, and more will I stimulate

A reasonable growth level can only be determined by me
Even a success echelon can only be set by me
A winner mentality can only be actualized by me
Even a champion mindset has to be erected by me

As I worried less about past mistakes
They unconsciously positioned as a stepping-stone
I know we meditated on a better day
But I'm sure faith and effort secured the pay.

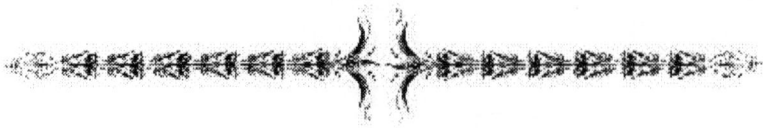

Confirmation

In a way,
Tomorrow's destination has been confirmed to us,
In response to today's magnificent performance.
In a way,
Future's doors are widely opened to us,
In response to how hard we knock today.
In a way
When the appointed time for materialization arrived,
Your age was not even in consideration.
In a way
When the actualization and materialization time
Of that person, before formation, He called
Legendary showed up, all goliaths vamoosed.

In a way,
A towering goal has been chosen by you,
As a result of excluding the useless.
In a way,
A grand style has been selected by you,
In agreement with a heavenly order.
In a way,
An undisputed elegance has been bestowed upon us
In confirmation of what I planned for myself and household;
For in the right hand of God's righteousness shall we conceal
ourselves.

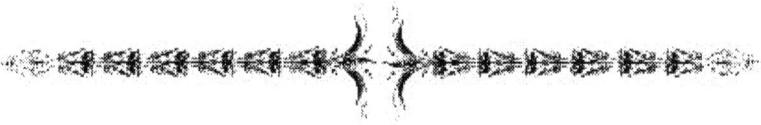

Undeniably Wrong

It is a shame
To recognize,
It is an abomination to the core
To realize,
Oh yes, It is repugnant to the extreme
To internalize
That some successful people
Aren't even aware of their great success,
That those whom it has been given care less,
And those who really need it never pray and plan,
That pessimism is, for some, a choice
Over optimism,
That animal rights have overtaken
Human rights,
That great men and women increasingly
Settle for a compromise,
That some people have been called children of God
Even when they utterly abhor peace,
That a good child has been asked not to pray
In an environment that requires prayer most,
That a lovely woman has continuously been told to plow
Without a tool,
In some forgotten areas, many good people have been left to
drink
The unsafe,
In a favored community, many people have been taught how
to plant and water a good seed.

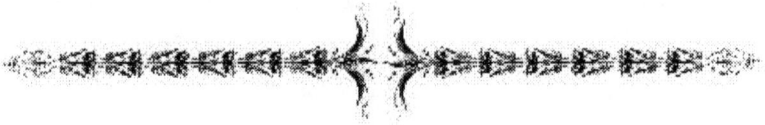

Elevation

So secured,
Like a baby in a mother's arm,
Feeling an exceptional fortification,
Accepting an exceptional proposition,
Carefully
Enveloped with a special kind of love,
Cautiously
Held in a special kind of way,
My God is
Carefully setting me up as a ray
Of hope,
He is gloriously lighting my beam of radiant energy,
A magnificent show of concrete validity,
Saturating
Me with His peace,
Protecting
Me with His power,
Pulling
Me safely from a dangerous zone,
Preparing
Me surely as a corner stone,
The doors of my comprehension
Have been widely opened for smooth entrances,
So often
Has the devil thought that I am weak,
Many times
Has he approached with a worn out technique
And secrets that heaven has already leaked,
I'm so grateful to trinity,
I'm so thankful to good people too,
Overly optimistic that my faith is my key,
Exceedingly hopeful that my prayer is my worry-free input,
I will prudently press on for my crown,
I will honestly embrace no let down.

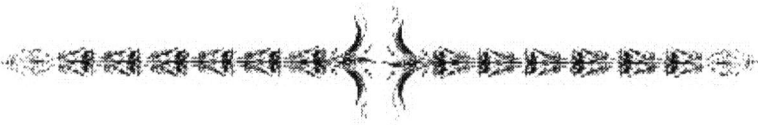

Nobody Has It All

Talk less about your help to others,
Gossip no more about your services to another.
Converse intensively about the aid you received,
Explain beyond qualm the good gifts gained from some folks.

No gift holds more dignity,
None holds more distinction,
Than that given on the cross,
Than that given to save us.

I feel good this afternoon,
The free of charge morning rain has left our
Environment looking clean and cool;
It even readied our soil for planting.

I couldn't pay for air
If God attaches a price tag to air,
Nor could I pay for love & protection,
Nor could I pay for peace & direction.

I asked for this day,
God gave me these days.
I prayed for daily bread,
God gave me an unspeakable joy that's full of glory.

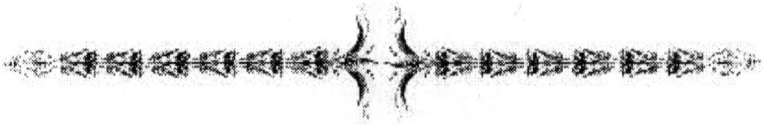

Reminisce

Early morning song, an early morning preaching in Africa
Loud as could be
Piercing through the morning dew,
Echoing through the quiet road of Clifford
The preacher's perspective seemed to declare
How great it will be someday
When vain men boast no more about their might
When ineffective people brag no more about their gifts
For the Nebuchadnezzar of Babylon
Boasted without God, crawled in pain

Early morning praise, early morning worship in an Africa
street
Clamorous as could be
Thundering through a shot window
Rumbling through a street I remembered
The preacher's teaching appeared to confirm
How magnificent it will be
When men brag only in the lord
When women boast only in the lord
For King David of Israel
Boasted in the lord that giveth all things

Early morning church, an early morning service in an
African street
Strident as could be
Penetrating through my precious soul
Hitting hard at my thought depot
The preacher's points concurred my opinion
How glorious it will be
When cities and states elect God fearing fellows

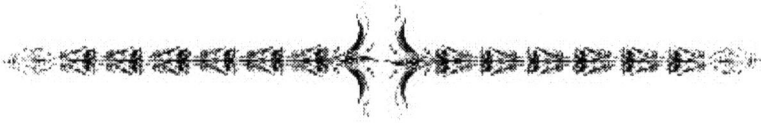

When nations and continents elect God fearing citizens
For God fearing people
Are people of equity, Are people of harmony.

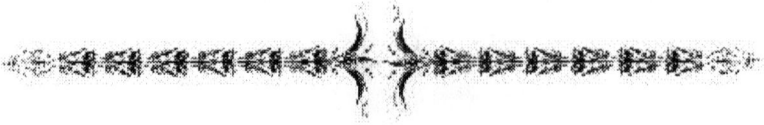

Uniqueness

He is not more intelligent than you
Just Different
She is not more sagacious
Just different as made
He is not better than you
Just different
She is not more superior
Just different as made
He is not more striking than you
Just different
She is not prettier
Just different as made
He is not more charismatic than you
Just different
She is not more appealing
Just different as made
He is not more articulate than you
Just different
She is not more logical
Just different as made
He is no better manager than you
Just different
She is no better organizer
Just different as made.

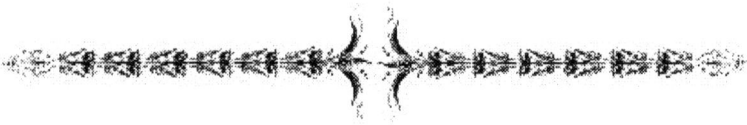

Benefits of Love

show me the fields of love so I may plow too
for blessed are those who stand out rain or shine
to accommodate those positive uniqueness
of fellow mankind as not forbidden by God,
for others and the Creator will likewise
contain their positive differences.
blessed is that organization
that tolerates those unique
attributes as encouraged by God
for such will inevitably reap from the
principles of diversity and the principles of
of division of labor, even, as apostle Paul stated.
for such will also harvest from the principles of loving
thy neighbors, principles of living in harmony, even, as Jesus
taught, even as Christ confirmed and indubitably practiced
satisfy my soul now and direct me to the fields of love so I
may sow too.

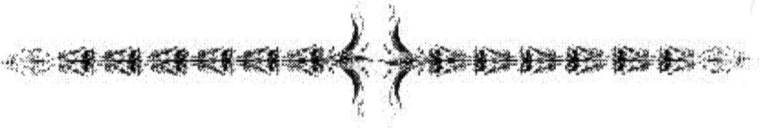

Presence

By His grace, your honor has been kept intact,
A covenant so right and so progressive,
An agreement so honorable and so impressive.
Those wrongs you forgave,
Those pressures you endured,
Suddenly, an intervention,
A God, A Father,
A reassurance,
A confirmation,
A simple accord expresses,
I will guide you if you acknowledge me.

Similar words heard before, comparable dreams,
Have today manifested vividly and garishly.
They manifested, and greatness is smoothly unboxed.
All obstacles that hated you have given up,
The hindrances on your way vamoosed and surrendered
And that huge block on the way
Altered to a stepping-stone.
Not many options were given to your adversaries
As a Father, A God
A Domination
Ruled
Through massive actions
Saying: I am Your God-Jehovah Nissi

Parallel love shown before through His authority
Has again evidenced so plain and so simple,
It evidenced, and beauty is released.
Even the weather took an order,
Not to be too hot or too cold on you.

A Father, A Jehovah Jireh
A weight
A Power,
Pressing on the rain of love to fall on you,
They're descending liberally to   soak you dearly.

A Good Boy's Unadulterated Prayer

His wish breezes like a spring in Alabama
His thoughts radiate like the full moon
His smile makes his family glad
His prayer cuts and draws high attention
Yet simple lines did he choose.

May the evil mongers disappear in haste
Vanish to oblivion
Fade away to a bottomless pit
Evaporate like gas
Wane to nothing

May the chasers of goodness show up in style
Come out for peace
Approach for togetherness
Draw near for love
Get closer for positive growth.

May the workers of decency
Accept their roles
Help the younger ones
Instruct them about prayer, faith, and planning
Instill in them hope, love, and peace.

Surely, like a spring in Alabama his wish breezes
Like a full moon his thoughts radiate
Like a charm his smile lures
Like a magnet his prayer draws
Still uncomplicated lines did he prefer.

30

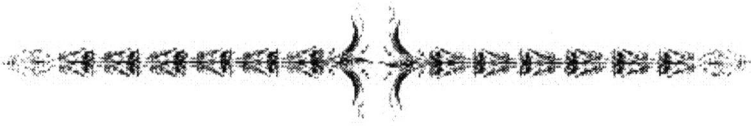

Classy Christian Family

Who said you are not so royal
Who said you are not so much
You are a classy Christian family
You are more than just a regular family
Without an artificial fertilizer your faith grows
Because nourishment is rooted in the rock of ages
Like a knife your prayer cuts,
Because your God receives your prayer
Hoping and believing, you pray a lot
Procuring and acquiring, your faith is hot
Holding firm a God above all gods
Following a master that knows it all
Your table is always prepared
By a God you've always magnified
Like a dagger, your flair for God
Pierces through the devil's heart
Dressing and talking it, you love culture
Admiring and feeling it, you love nature too
Living and appreciating it, you love beauty
Approving and complimenting it, you love pretty too
In the church, when you think about God
And what He's done, you dance
At home, when you think about Jesus
And how He set you free
You've always danced and danced
Charismatic and enigmatic, you've bewildered
Charming and lovely, you've shared
Humble and exquisite, you've stunned
As the children of the King
You have a right and the key to the Kingdom
So who said you are not so royal
Now who said you are not so much?

31

Two Kinds Of People

A researcher has deteriorated his principles by questioning
creation
A creature has devalued his integrity by questioning human
formation
A being has diminished his intellect worrying about man's
origin
Often a question arises, creating chaos in our lives
Often we must ignore, so often we must accept
Things that we cannot change

An individual has injured his cleverness wondering about the
created
A person has screwed up completely working to classify
beings
Someone has shrunk in magnitude trying to figure God's
intention
Often our curiosity rages, causing confusion in our lives
Often we must neglect, so often we must focus only on
Things that we can change

A creator, undoubtedly, created two types of people
An omniscient God positively fashioned two forms of people
An all-knowing God indubitably designed two kinds of people
Often our inquisitiveness ransacks, creating problem for us
Often must we accept, so often must we accept that
He made just Adam and Eve, A man and a woman;
Whom I know not their colors.

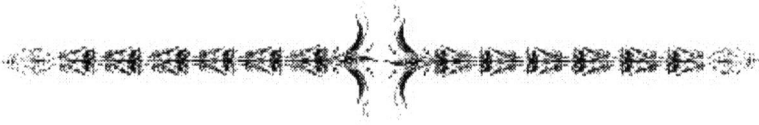

Udo's Pen

My pen has received an order from God
An instruction from Jesus
A directive from the Holy Spirit
A message from the angels
A communication from heaven.

A prayer from my family
A mandate from my conscience
A plan from the meek
A specification from the gentle
A condition from the young
An authority from the elders.

A command from the peacemakers
A stipulation from the forgotten
A pattern from the winners
A signal from good men
A nod from good women.

A decree from the commoners
A support from all God's children
A guideline from the word of God
To encourage, to stir up, and to motivate.

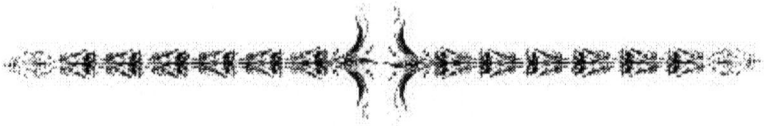

It Takes More Than Wishes and Thinking

Like sharp knives, these questions pierce and slice
From east to west they pierce
From north to south they slice
Like storms, these questions rage and wrath
From a coastline to a shoreline they rage
From down line to top line they conquer
Can wishes alone guarantee success?
If wishes alone guarantee success
Every body is then a success
Everybody wishes and I'm sure
Can thinking by itself turn things around?
If thinking by itself will move a mountain
All mountains would have been moved
Every body thinks and I'm sure
Can throwing ball a few hundred times make one a
professional?
If just throwing a ball few times makes a professional
Every body would have been professionals
Every body has thrown ball a few times and I'm sure
Can playing games in the computer make you a computer
specialist?
If playing a game makes a programmer
A lot would have become specialists
For many plays and I'm sure
Can dreaming alone make you a star?
If dreaming alone makes a star
The world would have been saturated with stars
Everybody dreams and I'm sure
The exclusion of the unwanted it requires
The inclusion of the needed it entails
For the exclusion of negative distraction it takes
And the inclusion of the positive energy it demands
As success rummages around and about
Around for prayer, action, persistence, and determination.

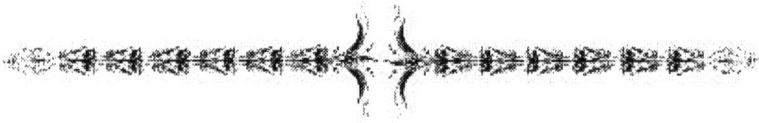

What You Sow Is What You Reap

True For Joseph in Bible, a forgiver
His focus, his favor
True for Joseph's siblings, the connivers
Their envy, their fall

Certain for David, a favorite
His gratefulness, his glory
Certain for Goliath, the vain
His pride, his collapse

Sure for the forces of darkness
Their evil, their pain
Sure for the good people
Their works, their throne

A fact for Cornelius, the helper
His seeds, his recognition
A fact for Pharaoh, the stubborn
His weird inflexibility, his drown

Definite for Abraham, a preferred
His faith, his favor
Good for Daniel, a believer
His devotion, his deliverance

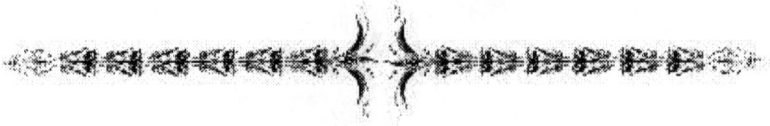

Appreciation

My morning is bright and clear
My songs so sweet in the ear
Lord I thank you, good Lord I praise you

My God has done the filtering
Good family, nice friends to cling
Lord I thank you, good Lord I praise you

The God of my family
Has done it again and again
Lord I thank you, good Lord I bless you

Discouragement has become encouragement forever
Moods of despair utterly diminished
Lord I thank you, good Lord I thank you

The presence of less was temporary
The company of more is permanent
Lord I thank you, good Lord I worship you

I can fly as far as I desire
Soaring and staying in the middle
Of my guiding angels, good Lord I adore you.

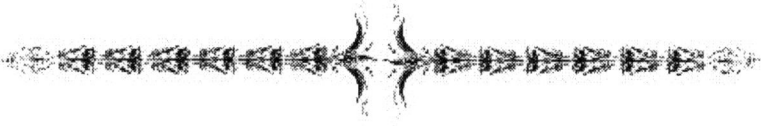

Hallelujah

Workers of iniquity always evaporate
When God's children celebrate.
Lord, I salute you-- hallelujah

The devil and company will vacate
When faith's energy we activate.
Lord, I salute you--hallelujah

Forces of darkness I exterminate
As my prayer slashes and intimidates.
Lord, I salute you--hallelujah

Rulers of murkiness will evacuate,
As their evil deeds we humiliate.
Lord I salute you--hallelujah

Sessions of doom will obliterate
When hate and wars we eradicate and terminate.
Lord, I salute you--hallelujah

God's mercy has advocated
Eliminated, annihilated, and elevated
Lord I salute you--hallelujah

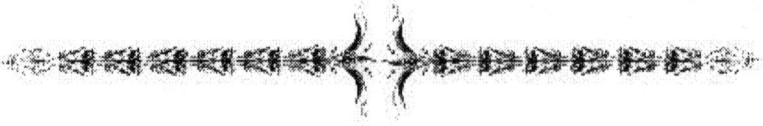

You'll Overcome

You will overcome,
Your stars of hope shine brightest,
Exposing an evil intended gathering.
Your great God controls your stars and paths
As you triumph in your good deeds and efforts
Rejoicing, praising, for the good tidings
Has announced, assured, and reassured.
Those hands that try to push you down,
Will inevitably salute your good works.
That mouth that spoke you down,
Will inescapably speak you up.
Those ears that close at your name's call
Will yearn eagerly to hear your name.
That door that closes at your face
Opens wide at the first knock
Cash then scarce in your wallet
Will fight for a space as you overcome.
Those fellows who keep you at miles' length
Will reach to hug you at yard's extent.
Even the devil that hated you with a passion
Will respect, flummox, and flabbergast at your action.
He will be stunned by an endeavor packed with prayer, plan,
faith, and hard work.

Unworthy Interference

Sometimes,
We bring our problems
For God to fix
Yet we interfere with our suggestion
Messing up an elucidation
Killing a divine solution
We could have let Him do it alone

From time to time
Ezekiel will bring his home work for my help
Honestly trusting my competence
But my judgment will he question
Unknowingly attacking a dear confidence
Just raising unnecessary concern
He could have done it himself

Every so often
We take it to the Lord in prayer
Laying it in His waiting arms
Still we worry to harm
Endangering a benefit
Setting unnecessary confusion
We could have let Him do it alone

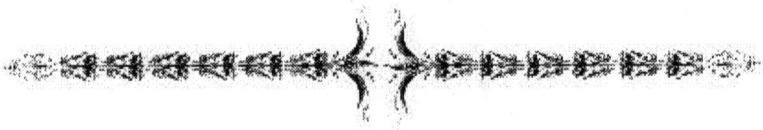

A Fantasy

It sounds like Udo & family
It's a beautiful island of Udorifamily
Where in harmony all live together
Where peace lovers parade with crowns
A place of serene fiesta
Where all God's children gravitate to the energy of true love
A land that's unendingly illuminated by the heavenly stars
A place I'll love to see Udorifamily
Take a break as Udo treats them
With those specials containing Udo's spice
Fish dishes with greens, pure juices and coconut rice
A place where in one accord all live mutually
Where peace and love are constitutional
Where envy and hatred are unconstitutional
I will love to hear them sing with the birds
I will like to intentionally forget those phone numbers
And passwords
In that lavish island of Udorifamily
With few days of no cry and no fuss,
We'll breathe the air of goodness
With songs of praise and not shitashita
We'll dance to a God of love
With songs of worship and not pitapita
We'll worship the Almighty above
Sip on spumante fre and pure iced water
It certainly will be much greater
Than previous adventures to see Udorifamily
Load quietness, love, for the island of Udorifamily

40

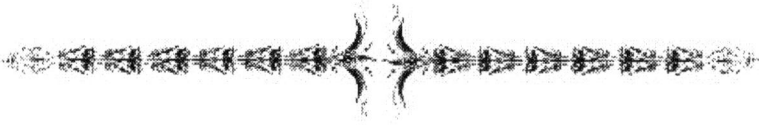

Life Is Meant To Be Challenging

Delight in those beauties around you,
Enjoy your life each day to the fullest.
There will always be a problem to solve,
For life is made to be challenging.

Dissect the expectations of life with vigor,
Confronting challenges with joy,
Approach difficulties with confidence,
For life is made to be challenging

Arrive at each step full of love
Have fun with positive things that life offers
Enjoying today and expecting a better tomorrow
For life is made to be challenging

Take pleasure in all goodness around you
Wait not for that big break before being happy
For after such break comes another challenge
For life is made to be challenging

My father in Heaven made this day
I'm going to have fun this day
After paying off that project, there will be another
For life is made to be challenging
For life is meant to be like that.

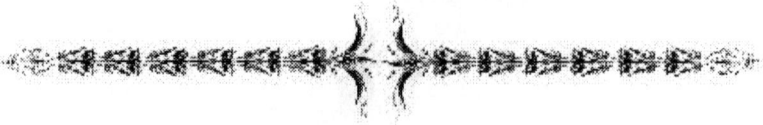

Soul Searching

Relaxing,
Meditating,
Thinking,
Asking,
And searching a good soul
Challenging a fine thought depot
Wanting to know more on perfection
Trying to hear more on flawlessness.
An influence rigmaroles my soul and seems to say
Perfection is nigh, Righteousness is here
Attainment is high, accomplishment is glory
Perfection is trinity, living right is human
God's righteousness you are, your righteousness is mucky.
Still relaxing,
Still meditating,
Still thinking,
Still asking,
A powerful voice penetrates my soul
And says, "Intentional mistakes are dishonorable,
And some unintentional slip-ups are disreputable
But as mistakes must occur in an imperfect world,
The effects of these mistakes are only determined by
What you do after such falls."

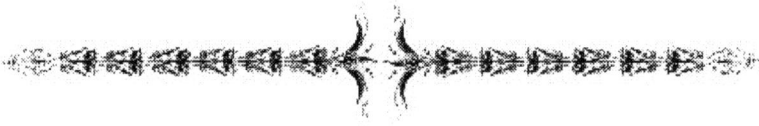

A Cry For Hope

I see something in the future
That is friendly to my thought
I even dreamt of a pattern in the future
That agrees with my hope.

Every body that wants happiness is happy
Everybody that wants success is successful
Everybody that wants peace is peaceful
Everybody that wants joy is joyful

I mean I see something in the future
That is compromising to my belief
I even hear of a pattern in the future
That agrees with my faith

All God's children coming together
All good people having enough to eat
All God's children having a shelter over their heads
All good people living in peace

I cannot wait any longer
And my soul is overly eager
Echoes of war vanishing forever
Foes of peace vamoosing to wherever.

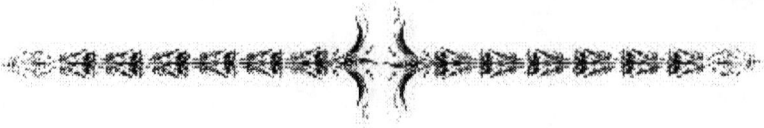

Diligence

Hard work teaches without compromise
A pen stirs up blood for motivation
Stirs up, stirs up, and mesmerizes

Word of God incessantly edifies
As Holy Ghost works at clarification
Works, works, and energizes

Today's good work surely glorifies
God and promotes elevation
Promotes, promotes, and unifies

Tomorrow's good work must emphasize
A total annihilation of human degradation
Annihilate, annihilate, and paralyze

Hard work won the prize
Meticulousness & diligence overpowered procrastination
Overpowered, overpowered, and justified

As God's anointing carefully intensifies
A humble heart enjoys a divine cooperation
Enjoys, enjoys, and multiplies

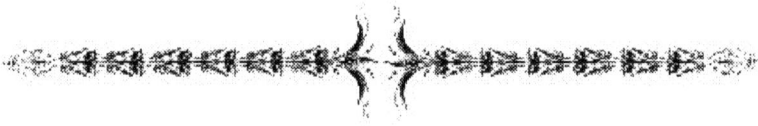

God is in My Plan

The dream of the righteous dieth not
Even though envy may lead to a plot
To God's plan we'll say thanks a lot

When you dreamt of your bundle of wheat
In the middle and others bowed to it
God was in the plan

When I dreamt of my river
Turning to ocean with varieties therein
God was in the plan

They think less about you
In a dry well in a promising county
God is in the plan

You think they betrayed you
By letting umbrage overtake them
God is in the plan

When your gift has not made a way yet
And you held to your faith
God is in the plan

When your gift finally made a way
And you thank and praise the source of the gift
Source of the gift is in the plan

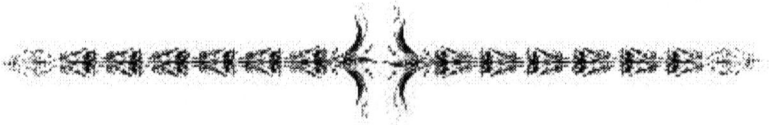

So Shall the Connection Be

In me
The devil saw a man made in God's image
So he panicked
Observing me relentlessly, he saw a juggernaut
So he feared
So he panicked, he feared, and he persecuted
So he feared, he persecuted, but I triumphed

A good
Person is asked to go to a place he or she is uncertain about
So he worries
But when God of Moses and Jonah shows up
So he startles
So he worries, he frightens and he obeys
So he frightens, he obeys, and he conquers.

When the
Time of interpreting and writing shows up
So his heart gladdens
So his heart gladdens and His God is smiling
So his heart gladdens, God is happy, but the devil is angry
So his God rejoices, he praises and celebrates

When God's
Appointed time arrives
Shut doors open wide
When a mighty rod hits the sea blocking your journey
The Sea divides into two
The shut door opens, and the blocking sea divides
The door opens, the blocking sea divides and makes a way.

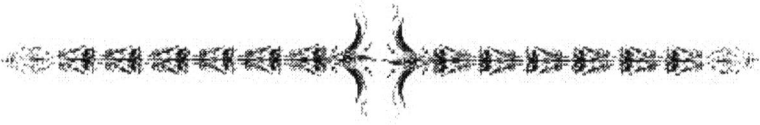

Responsibility

Be slow
To negative thoughts of rejection
Be fast
To acknowledge God in storms midst
Be unhurried
With feelings of abandonment
Be quick
In recalling favors
Be sluggish
In recollecting past mistakes
Be hasty
In thanking God for everything
Be sluggish
In using up your patience
Be indolent
In apportioning blames
Be persistent
Your first shipment is ready to unload
Be strong
For your second shipment is near the wharf
Please be determined in your prayer
For the third shipment has just blasted off.

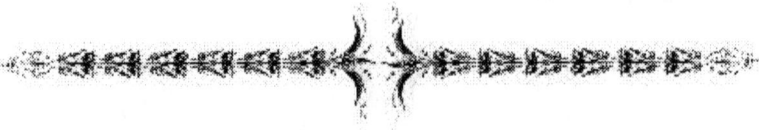

My Total Prosperity Strategy

My soul longs to perpetuate this intense feeling of gratitude
to the only God that deserves unreserved credit
My heart seeks out the basics for excellence
And a heart now rejoices
Most times when I ask Jesus for prosperity strategy
He refers me to Luke 6:38
Sometimes He refers me to 2 Corinthians 9:6
My mind asks the Omniscience for guidance
And a mind obviously relaxes
Most times when I ask God for a financial plan
He refers me to Malachi 3:10
Sometimes He refers me to Malachi 3: 11-12
When I wonder what God thinks about my total plan
Most times He refers me to 3 John 1:2
Sometimes He refers me to Isaiah 1:19
He even tells me to knock and it shall be opened
So my hand knocks on all viable options
And the doors are opening
And the locks are unlocking
My air is so fresh
My water is so pure
My loving gets so enhanced
And my Redeemer lives
My financial pharaohs have taken to their heels
I have waited upon the Lord
My strength is renewed
My perception is positive
All enemies are running to a point of no return
Some, I know how
Some, I don't know how
But one thing that I know is that
My sun shines for its role
And my rain falls for its duty

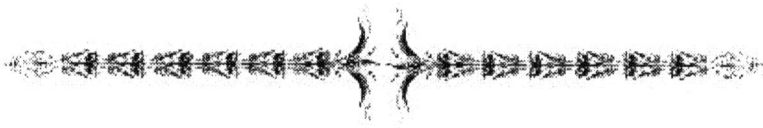

My job is enriching
My business is expanding
My God reigns forever
My financial darkness has taken to its heels, I repeat
As a faith drew strength and might
I never imagined a quick manifestation of God's glory
I must confess
An entrance to greatness is all I see
An embodiment of goodness is all I hug
I glorify The Most High for unlocking the locks
Be magnified Lord for opening a new axis
For which my warm heart embraces
Forgive us for worrying about closed doors
Instead of rejoicing for open doors
For precious energy expended on closed doors
Has distracted the light, the beauty, the dignity,
And the honor of a widely opened door.

Graceful Aging

Like a house,
Their value appreciates as the year goes by
Like well watered gardens
They flourish as the time goes by
As trees planted by the riverside
Their leaves remain green as fruits abound
Like homes built on solid ground
The storm avoids them
Like God fearing people
Their relationship with the almighty gets better
Their hugs get warmer
Their words get more encouraging
Outward beauty smartly transfers
Itself to the inside
They remaineth beautiful as time goes by
They remaineth gorgeous till the last day
As a face in some areas wrinkle
The inside in all areas sparkle
Their truth gets truther
As their love gets lovelier
Their smile gets prettier
As their hug gets warmer and warmer.

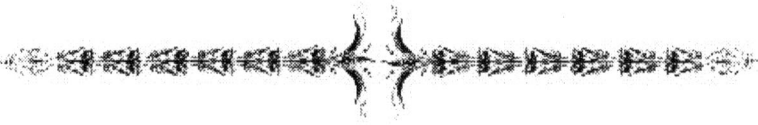

Worthy Period

A worthy period appears
Very long
For the impatience
Very boring
For the intolerable
Very rushed
For those who plan not
Very confused
For those who pray not
Very frustrating
For those who share not
Very sluggish
For those who love not
Very agonizing
For the wickedly wicked
Very prolonged
For wrong celebrations
Very short
For meaningful celebrations
Very pleasant
For good people
Very appealing
To nice people
Very precious
For the joyful
Always very short
For meetings of good intention.

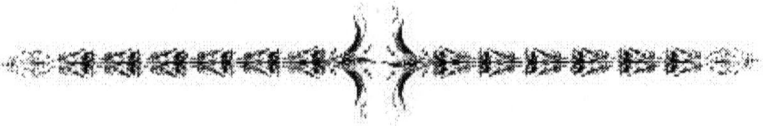

Credit Card

Know ye that
It is incorrect to live on credit card
If you have the cash
Your joy it may steal
Children's future it may filch
Your investments it may snatch
Your total joy may be affected

Recognize ye that
It is honorable to have good credit
Your dignity does it identify
Low interest rates may it secure
Fine home purchase may it aid
New business acquisition may it assist
Reduced aggravation may it enhance

Know ye that
It is wrong to live on credit card
If you have the hard moolah
Your good seeds may it steal
Your offerings may it seize
Your tithe may it influence
A good harvest may it affect

Recognize ye that
It is honorable to have good credit standing
Your excellent reputation may it secure
Sharing may it facilitate
Loving may it smooth the progress of
Your business growth may it aid
Self-confidence it will instill

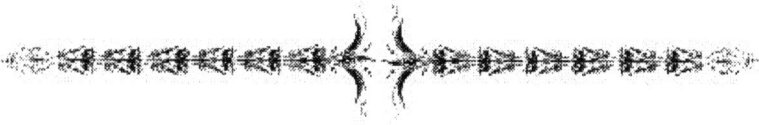

Know ye that
It is dishonorable to live on credit card
If you have the dough
A marriage may it affect
A business may it destroy
A honey may it steal
A body may it stress

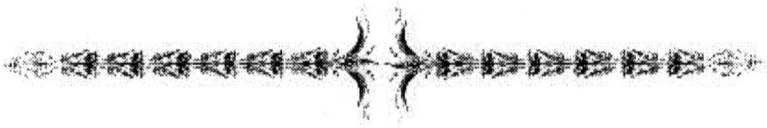

Be Not Wise Only In Your Own Eyes

But for how long can a good person
Pretend to know it all
For even Pele, Michael Jordan, and J. Montana
Took advice from their coaches

But for how stretched can a good quality person
Pretend to be perfect
For such deception takes away the
Energy so needed for striving for perfection.

But to what extent will that person
Pretend not to know that my God is able
For such pretense is as good as being blind
For such pretense is a direct child of stubbornness

But for how long shall we pretend not to see these hostilities
Sensitivity must boldly challenge insensitivity
A superior move must defy an inferior move
Oh yes, Good thoughts must continue to confront bad
thoughts.

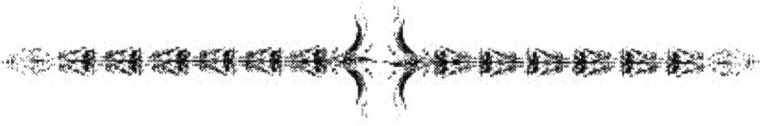

You Are Blessed

Your pessimism constantly strikes a tune
That vibrates in my soul.
You have not looked
To your front or to your back
Lately, this tune vigorously relates.
Constantly piling pressure on a mind so decent
A silly way to torment God's gift.
You have not looked
To your left or to your right
In recent times.
Incessantly loading stress on a heart so pure,
An absurd way to agonize something special.
To your front and to your back
People are definitely worse off than you,
To your left and to your right
People are seeking what you already have.
You are a child of God
Which secured you a right in God's kingdom
You have the connection to Joydom
You are happy, and the body of Christ is happy too
And you wonder if you are extremely successful.
You have access to the pure water well
And you wonder if you are immensely blessed
You must have not looked to your
Front and back lately
You must have not counted your
Blessings lately
You must not have excluded the unwanted
newly
And you must not have included the needed
Recently.

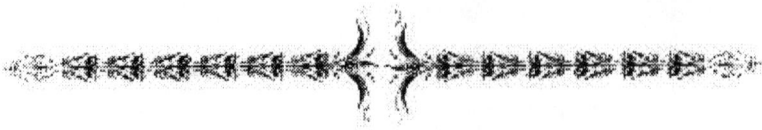

I'm the Best in God's Eyes

I mean not to be arrogant at all
But I must perpetuate this great understanding
And enhance the continuous flow of my river of joy
For I'm still the best in God's eyes
I call not my self-egotistical of course
I'm not trying to prove anything you know
I'm only a manifestation of what God knew
Before I was formed
To the highest prize have I set my eyes
No other than me deserves the greatest size
I hold tight to the promise of a Father
Who guaranteed me the good of the land
If I'm willing and obedient
Who promised to show me things that I've not before seen
If I call upon him
Who promised to fulfill all my good desires
For accepting His son as a savior
Who promised to open my door
If I knock
Who promised to bless my descendants and me
As a favored son
I vowed not to settle for good when best is nigh
As a favored son
I vowed to praise and worship the lord
With my household
As a favored family
We vowed to serve the lord
For as long as we live.

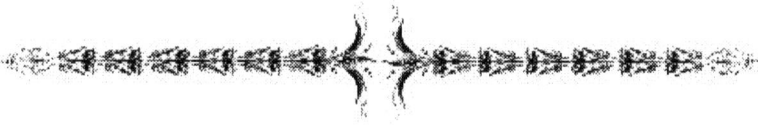

Fallen Goliaths

A precious light
An unquenchable light
A precious light has been my guide
To all touch downs, to all crowns

Bye to worry, bye bye to vex
The joy of the lord has become our vigor
As we acquire, as we conquer
As we watch our barn crammed and running over

Bye bye to fear, bye bye to procrastination
For the work of God is manifested
To a large scope, to a great extent
For a dangerous python lies without a head

Love and favor, peace and joy
The ills flushed to nonexistence
With all dejection we flushed, washed out with all rejection
The mountain of obstruction is melted and melted down.

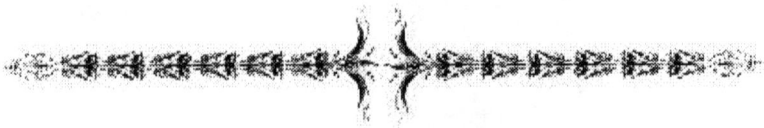

Tied Impediments

Your impediments have been tied
Obviously hostaged and petrified
For all reliable evidence so implied
To all impediments brushed to the roadside
Including, but not only, vain pride.
Even Stagnancy, anger, and mediocrity were defied
Oh yes your impediments
Of idleness, of slow growth, of inadequacy complex, of bad
Credit, of avariciousness, cupidity, debts, have been tied
Oh yes your impediments
Of no husband, of no child, no wife, of sickness
Have been tied
Oh yes your Pharaoh
Of low morale, of not getting good feelings,
Of I cannot do it, of stress, of lack, of hopelessness is tied.
Hindrance has been tied, as a bundle of pain is gone to
oblivion
Encumbrance has been openly defied in a fierce contest
And you owe no debt any more
Oh yes your impediment
Received an ultimatum as bondage is tied
Received a reminder for all debts paid
On the cross of Calvary.

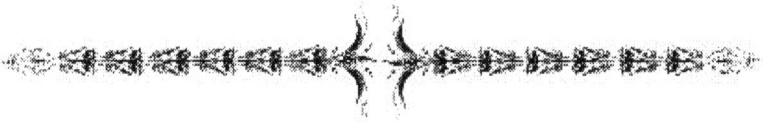

Lead Me in Style

Lord
When I show up in informal occasions
When I show up in formal occasions
When I show at up at work
May you lead me in style

Lord
When I show up in church
When I show up in a conference
When I show up in a meeting
May you lead me in style

Lord
When I show up among believers
When I show up among non-believers
When I show up in a family gathering
May you lead me in style

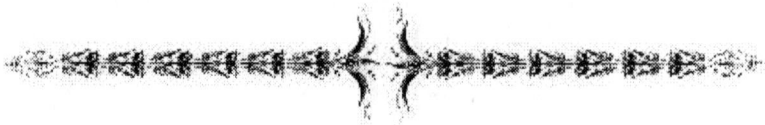

A Sexy Christian

At home, your energy is so recognized
At work your faith has often mesmerized
You are so focused, and you've not even realized
Just a superior connection has made you more classy
You don't even need more junk to be essentially sexy
Your confidence
Your common sense
Your resents
Is sexy sexy
The way you sing
The way you bring
The way you cling
You're just a sexy Christian
The way you smile
The way you reconcile
The way you style
You're just a sexy Christian
The way you spirit dance
The way you folk dance
The way you image-enhance
You're just a sexy Christian
The way you understand
The way you stand
The way you demand
You're just a sexy Christian
The way you clap
The way you rap
The way you tap
You're just a sexy Christian
The way you pray
The way you play
The way you say
It's just Christian sexy

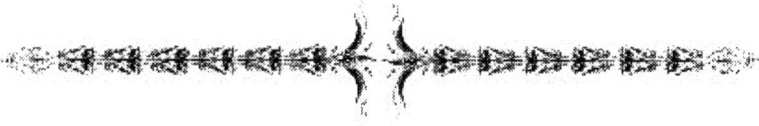

The way she phrases
The way she amazes
The way she praises
It's just sexy sexy
Just a sexy Christian.

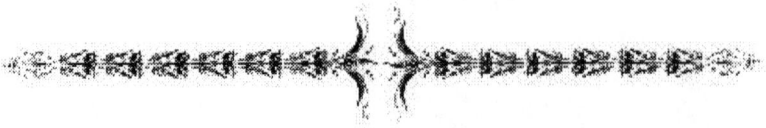

I Want to Love You More Than I Need You

My inside has spoken loudly
The truth has refused to lie low
My heart pressures me indeed
I want to love you more than
I need you

Your gestures have spoken loud too
The truth must sooner be uncovered
Your expression signals my intellect
You too want to love me more than
You need me

Honestly, my within is energized intensively
The truth insists in coming out
My spirit is excessively and exceptionally eager
I want to love you more than
I need you

For such love have I yearned for too long
For such love have you longed too delayed for
Our insides compel us indeed
Our hearts pressure us too much
To love each other more than we need each other.

Errand and Resources

Lord
You told me to sow and water
You gave me a good seed
You told me to write
You overwhelmed me with resources
You asked me to sweep
You handed me a broom
You sent me to the mall
You gave me cash not card
You told me to be a father, a husband, and a brother
You provided me a bible
You gave me a job
You gave me a tool
You told me to praise you
You gave me voice
You gave me hands too
My praise is become a magnet
My prayer is become a link
And the Holy Spirit has arranged my seed box
With my seed box packed and set
I procrastinate no more and I defer no longer
I am on my way to a fertile place
My bible is become my compass too
My worship is become a lure also
My praise will remain a duty
And this duty will remain my puller.

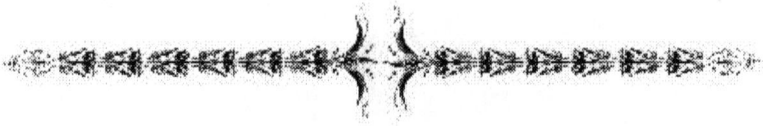

Confidence Attacks

Let your confidence attack
Confidence will attack
As your God directs your footstep.
For what the interviewer wants,
You are
Believe in your ability
Trust in the power of prayer
And let confidence attack
Confidence must attack
Attack like a shark after blood.
Listen for a divine voice
And let obedience attract
Obedience surely attracts
And draws like a magnet.
The good in you has risen to eclipse the imperfection
Your best will emerge to overshadow all deficiency
Your faith in God assures
As you make that appointment
Showing up in confidence
Getting ready to obey a meaningful order
Believing that days of hostile work environment
Are over
Oh yes and a better paycheck
Oh yes and a better benefit
Oh yes a quality time for family
Oh yes a renewed energy for praise, prayer, and worship.

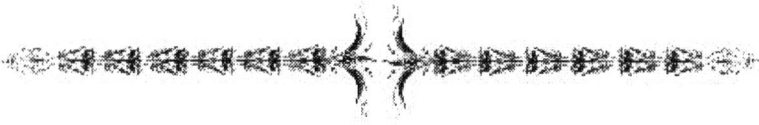

Shine

You are a city on a mountain
A light powered by trinity
The devil stunned and bewildered today
Will be astonished and verily astounded tomorrow
For regrets over trying to quench a light rooted on solid rock.
The devil owes for getting your attention
The devil did not like you then
The devil does not like you now
for your kind of light never quenches absolutely
The devil will always respect you
The devil will always revere you
If you shine according to plan
Thou will become a source for others
If you shine according to plan
Thou will become a model for others
If you shine according to plan
Thou will become a city on a mountain
If you shine according to plan
Thy cup will be full and running over
If you shine according to plan
Thy barn will be filled with harvest
If you shine according to plan
Thy joy will be unspeakable
If you shine according to plan
Thy joy will be full of glory
If you shine according to plan.

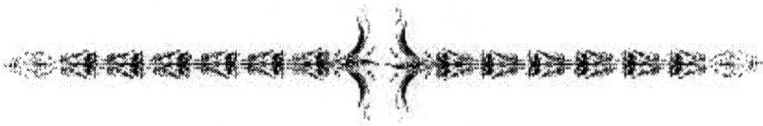

Radiant Energy From Heaven

An energy beaming to conquer,
A vigor glowing to surmount
A dynamism gleaming to prevail

No lid covereth a boiling anointing
No one hideth a city on a mountain
And no devil devoureth a seed with divine protection

A force shinning to consume evil plans
A vitality radiating to triumph over iniquity
A vigor roaring to accomplish a delightful mission

No one can impede our progress now
No human can stop a God's predestined
And no mortal can stop this divinely programmed

Our pressure is too much and gracefully protected
Our force is plenty and exquisitely covered
In Jesus name, no one can stop us now.

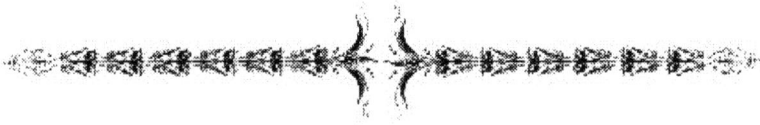

Include the Needed

Procrastination and discouragement
Now fearlessly trashed
And boldly abandoned,
Have given spaces
To diligence and encouragement.
Industrious and assiduous
Now audaciously embraced
Have taken up seats
For fear of failure.
God's favor and honor
So divinely bestowed
Have given rooms
To conquests and victories.
Those wants not good for me
Have been excluded
To include the needed.
Chosen to brighten brightly,
Selected to inspire vehemently.
Each time a good deed is accomplished,
My light is felt.
Every time we sow a good seed,
Our light is perceived.
Thank God for darkness
Impudently excluded, giving way
For brightness to consume massively
And perpetuate a gleaming ray of hope
For the optimistics and all the expectants of goodness.

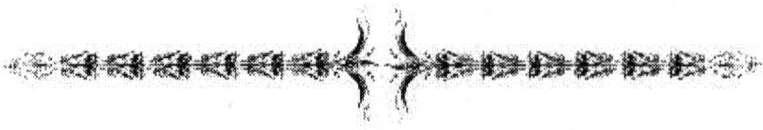

Goodness And True Love

Good things said before,
Are being said now,
And will be said again.
Being said about true love,
Will be said again
About peace and love.
Has been said before
About goodness and compassion.
For it is no fallacy that a man
Of peace and harmony is a
Man of enormous chances.
For it is no lie that
A woman of faith is
A woman with unlimited boundaries.
For it is no misleading notion that
A good child maketh his parents proud
But a bad child pierces a parent 's heart
With a blunt and rusted dagger.
Tell not your parents that you love them
If you intentionally disobey their commandments.
Tell not your children that you love them,
If you calculatedly degrade and mislead them.
For true love is like pure water
It does not degrade, it surely upgrades.
It's an aid, far better than Gatorade.
It invigorates, it's pure water, not lemonade.
It flushes the unwanted, it quenches the thirsty.
Even when the storms pressure we cannot bear,
True love is all we need.
Even when your bills you cannot pay,
True God will always show a way.
Even when peer pressures work to misinform,
True love will properly inform.

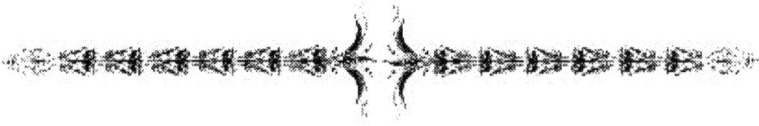

Even when bad company works to deceive
True love will work to straighten.
Even when a devil thinks you don't know
True love will comfort an ego
Even when some things look discouraging around us,
True love will fix them and make us hopeful
Even when they beat you to keep you down,
True God will transform that experience to a colossal
strength.

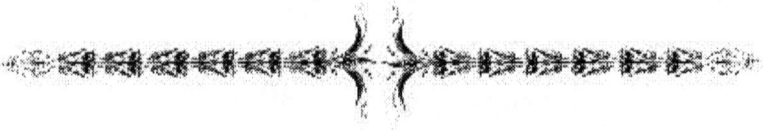

Heavenly Father

How beauteous His visits have been
How magnificent His touches have felt
Visits with gifts asked for
Visits with gifts not asked for
Healing touches requested for
Healing touches not even requested for
How liberally these gifts are bestowed
How bountifully these favors are showered

How splendid a care it has been
How impressive a love it has been
A care with a soothing palm
A care with a therapeutic balm
A love that counts no mistakes
A love that forgives an error
How compassionately this care has been delivered
How generously this love has been conveyed

He calls us His people
He calls us His children
He calls us the chosen
And He calls us His family
How generously this love has been conveyed
How compassionately this care has been delivered
How bountifully these favors are showered
How liberally these gifts are bestowed.

70

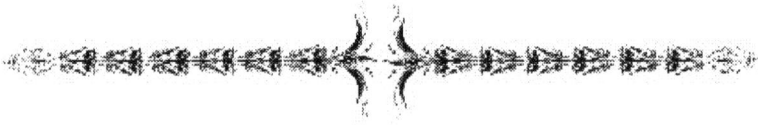

Give Normality A Chance

I'm favored
My eyes have seen the goodness of God
My ears have heard about the mighty works of God
My mouth will surely talk about the righteousness of God
Not mine
I've seen great leaves stayed green
In summer
They turned yellow, orange, & brown in due season
They've not become rigid
They've not become inflexible
They've changed color
In due season
They even fell on the ground
Giving way for a new season
Giving way for a new generation

We are favored
Our eyes will see the goodness of God
Our ears will hear about the mighty works of God
Our mouth will sing praises to our creator
Not ourselves
For the free air that we continually breathe
Year round came from an unselfish father
Of whom we are made like
We will not be stingy
We will not be tightfisted
We will not be a blockade
In a dutiful manner
Must we bless our offsprings
We will shepherd in the younger generation
And carefully guide out their younger innovation
As we permit their light to shine too.

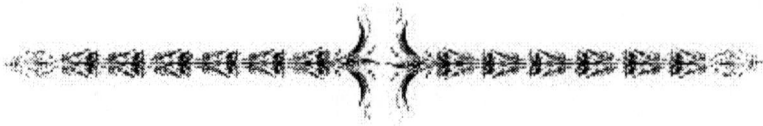

Extreme Success

Without God, it is no longer extreme success,
Deficient of the word of God, it lacks necessary nourishment,
And will die.
The best advice has been given to us,
We have heard the best recommendation today & before.
Obey and fear God
And wisdom is multiplied.
For how long will a person's potential
Remain obscured?
For how long will a seed with all prospective
Stay hidden?
Obey and fear God
And the good of the land will be yours
For a lively light is always powered
By a lively source,
For a vigorous light is always fueled
By an active base.
Oh yes many lights have quenched,
Consequent to suppressing God's anointed,
Oh yes many illuminations have extinguished
Ensuing from rebelliousness against God's people.
Many lights have reduced
Resulting from their unwillingness
To activate their blessing.
How rewarding it was for Abraham,
How gratifying it was for a father of all nations.
How worthwhile it will be too, if we comply.
So father, here we come
Eyes set on high
Pleading and praying for the anointing
To discern the most high voice,
For we are very willing
And candidly eager
To eat the best of the land.

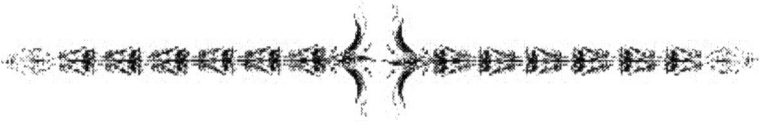

Victor Mentality

A resemblance of an impediment,
Like a Jericho wall from far and near,
A symbol of obstruction,
Moreover, a symbol of victory.
It was a Jericho wall that my
Heart was fixed to bulldoze.
My heart was fixed to conquer,
And everything was utterly conquered.
My faith was, and is still, my weapon.
My prayer was, and is still, my ammunition.
My praise and worship were, and are still, my weapon.
I heard a command that was in accord to my faith,
And I obeyed,
Then I conquered.
Yes, I will stay connected with this Commander,
For with This Commander, I have advanced against
hundreds,
For with This commander, I know that I will advance against
thousands.
Yes, I will remain loyal to this God,
For with this God, I have scaled a hill,
For with this commander, I know that I will scale a mountain.
Connected, yes, I will stay connected,
I am well positioned and related,
My hands are still up and up,
I have surrendered all and all,
Unadulterated humility has paid well today,
And I still want the best tomorrow.
Fully charged, my praise and worship
Instruments are situated,
Wholly stimulated, my faith and prayer
Are strategically located,
To trample, acquire, and entirely procure.

73

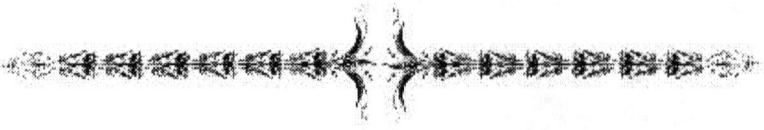

Real Praise and Worship

A clap, a song
A praise and worship so strong
The fire ferociously descended
Oh yes, and a dance in the spirit
Some smiled, some shed good tears
Then the devil got petrified
Haha, a mighty presence showed up
Aha, and all the demons got shook up
Hands raised, hope raised
Oh yes and a hearty prayer delivered
Some fell, some really fell
For the Holy Ghost was in charge
And the shamed devil was outdoors
Mighty name was faithfully hallowed
Suddenly, quietness followed
The Holy Spirit loudly spoke
Addressing a burdensome yoke
One voice, one interpreter
Oh yes the Lord has spoken to his people
Some spoke back to their heavenly father
In a language the devil could not decode
True peace they felt inside, as their exterior also glowed
Such a mighty presence it was then
Such a mighty presence it is now
Oh yes and a mighty presence in the future
That valid praise ushered a radiant presence of hope
The hearty worship pulled a beaming existence of trust
Oh yes and an unadulterated prayer ignited a fire of
deliverance.

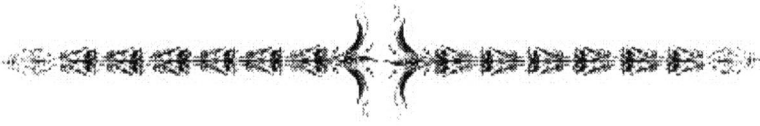

Knockdown, Not a Knockout

The beaten may have taken its toll
As those jabs on your faces land
Though on your knees you fell, looking up
It is a knockdown, not a knockout

Your energy wore thinner and thinner
But a voice whispers and whispers
Get up and exhibit your anointing
It is not over; it's just a knockdown

The value of your faith appreciates
Each time you block a shot
Every time you stagger up
All the time you stumble to your feet

When we fall down in a fight
Our choice reaches out to a favor or a failure
A choice to wise up, stagger up and triumph
Or a choice to look down, stay down as a looser.

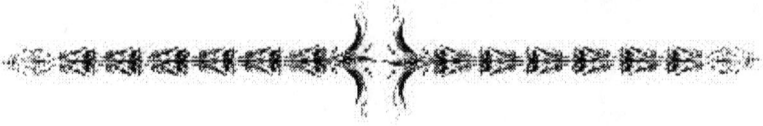

I'm Persuaded

I'm persuaded that the God of my parents
Will leave joy with me
At the crack of dawn

I'm convinced that the God of Abraham
Will honor my faith
And multiply my seeds

I'm swayed that the God of my children
Will call me His child
For peace fostered among His people

I'm certain that the God of Elijah
Will show up and devour
The output of iniquity

And I'm persuaded that the God of Udo & Rita
Will leave peace with my household
As He promised.

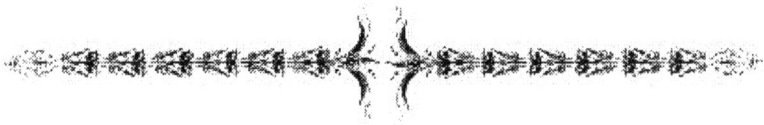

A Grateful Child's Song

A roof a roof a roof over my head
Daily bread daily bread daily bread always on our table
A God A God A God That's El-shaddai

Great angels great angels great angels all around me
A fence a fence a fence encircles me
A trinity a trinity a trinity that I'm proud to know

God's word God's word God's word is a light unto my path
Good book good book good bible has been my buddy
Our lord's prayer our lord's prayer a prayer so valuable t o
my memory

A faith a faith a faith that keeps us going
A prayer a prayer my prayer is a link to superior love
A love a love a love that is just supreme

He made a way, a way where devil thought there was no way
My alpha my alpha my alpha and Omega
Has done it has done it, has done just like He promised

Hallelujah hallelujah halle-lujah amen
Amen Amen Amen halle-lujah
Hallelujah hallelujah halle-lujah amen.

Simply Phat

It shines because it stays polished,
So burnished,
Sparkly, glittery, and glossy.
This car obviously makes my eyes happy each time.
This car often rides through a major boulevard,
This car is simply phat.
So expensive,
Costly, luxurious, and pricey.
I'm not jealous I must declare,
For in a pleasant county, God has blessed me
And I have bought some vehicles too.
But can we compare these vehicles to houses?
For these vehicles depreciate in values.
Can a cool car with splendid wheels become a reliable asset?
For cars deflate in value.
I care not to know who owns these phat cars,
For it is not personal, and will not be.
It may belong to a hard worker, a hopeful professional athlete,
A promising movie star, an expectant music star, or other.
For some of such people live in my region,
And many of these hopefuls read my books.
But one thing is obvious my friends,
But this fact have I proven fellow car lovers,
In the planning and setting up stages of your life,
It may be a blessing to drive a hooptie
Paid through hard work
Than to cruise your homeys in a pricey car,
And hassle grandma, mama, or grandpa so relentlessly,
For such style affects self-esteem,
A goal, a plan, and a future.
A good advice forever retains its value,
Drive it if you can afford it,

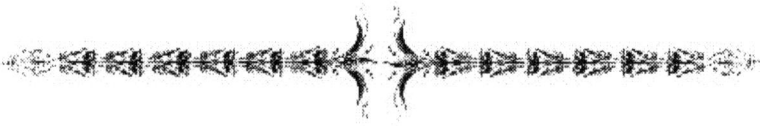

Cruise in it if you already have a place,
Enjoy it if it will not jeopardize your future
Because a star stuffed nature evaporates when foolhardiness
Gradually, steadily, and slowly mutilates.
Moreover, a star packed nature radiates when humbleness
Effectively, efficiently, and positively educates.

Forgiving Just Like That

But we must forgive,
Forgiveness, a key to Heaven's door
Forgetting, a balm for a war sore.
As we forgive not and hold deep grudges,
So do we not advance the cause of goodwill.
A true friendship may become negatively affected,
For the Holy Spirit may even be quenched in the process,
The mighty trinity may even be betrayed in the course,
As a good person could become vulnerable,
A divine favor possibly will become hugely affected.
As your true aficionados,
We'll try not to disappoint you.
We intend not to quench thee with gross unforgiveness.
How can we deliberately quench thee like that
Our dear comforter?
Knowing that you've been here
Each time we call,
You even came when we forgot to call.
How can I quench thee
Oh true advisor and intercessor?
Seeing that you interpreted when I couldn't
You led me to pure water wells
You fought my battles and defeated my foes
You led me to exclude the unwanted,
You directed me to include the needed
Just like that
Even when they demoralized me,
You comforted me,
Thou executeth righteousness and judgment your own way
Just like that
Please stay with me always,
My heart has become your address,
So I note down and know for a fact,

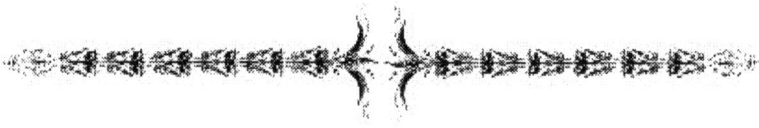

Thanks immensely for now,
Now that my youth is renewed like that,
Now that my strength is mightily rejuvenated,
Now that I'm ready to run and not be weary,
Now that I'm ready to walk and not faint,
Now that I'm revitalized enough for your orders,
Please stay perpetually, my true friend.
Just stay like that.

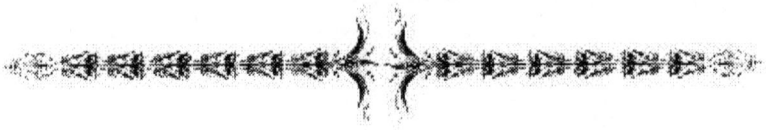

An African Civil War

The children knew not the cause
They were not in the negotiation meetings
The children knew not how it came to pass
But they absorbed the effects most
Hunger, anger, illiteracy, sickness, & death became the way.

A machine gun
A mortar
A shelling
A bomb
A missile
And a child became an orphan

A jet fighter flew so low
A bomber targeted even a moving goat
A jet bomber shot aimlessly at a church under a tree
A family separated painfully
Oh yes, and some children suffered kwashiorkor

A rage
A fear
A horror
A pain
A malnutrition
And a child too sick to smile

Neither school, nor book, nor love
Neither hospital, nor medicine, nor care
Neither bread, nor cheese, nor clean water
Lost sons, lost daughters, lost hope
Aha, and those families were left in sorrow

A Precious Birthday

The wise men came from the east;
they came looking for a newborn King.
The stars did they see and they came
To worship and to give.
Here we come today,
With pride,
Dignified,
As wise people,
To worship and to give.
As we worship and celebrate His birthday,
May we represent what He represents,
May we love all that Jesus loves:
Love, Peace, and Giving.

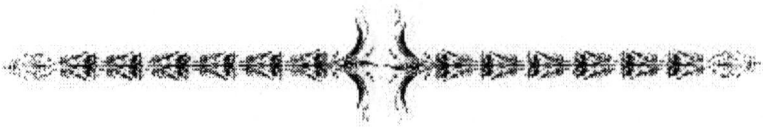

It's Up to You

The fire that you tried to extinguish
Is still burning and blazing
The pressure is on
The pressure is too much
The good thoughts that you tried to shun
Came raging towards you
The force is on
The force is too much
The good words that you tried to ignore
Came ringing in your ear
The power is on
The power is too much
The great plan that you spurned
Is coming your direction
The speed is high
The tempo is too high
Your Creator that you overlooked
Still has His hands opened
His arms are warm
His embrace is peace
And His hug is joy.

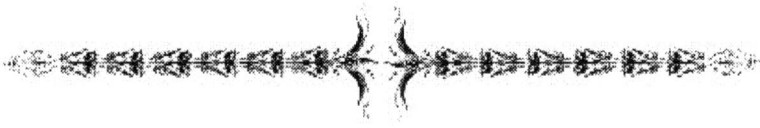

Thou Sayeth

I call not myself a philosophical juggernaut
For a philosophy may become just a viewpoint
I call not myself a research genius either
For a research may become just a good book
I call myself a man who seeks wisdom from God
A man whose faith cometh by hearing God's word
A man whose light is fueled from above
A man whose energy is from the main source

My bible has become my barometer
I care no more about gauging the atmospheric pressure today
I care no more to know from whence cometh my rain and sun
tomorrow
For my rain is controlled
For my sun is controlled
My Father in Heaven sends them
When my soil needs them
And when my plants require them.

I call not myself the analytical maestro or a great thinker
For God's thoughts have established my peace
I call not myself a perfectionist either
For the law of the Lord is perfect
I'll never call myself the offender
For the forgiver is become the strategically
Positioned receiver
That person whose light is fueled from above
That person whose energy is from the main source.

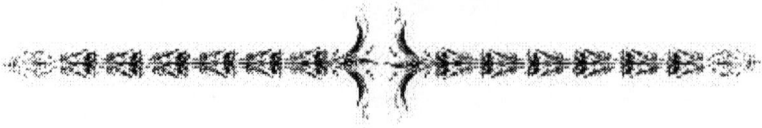

Praising Like No Man's Business

Even when I slide right bound
I'm praising Him in the spirit
When I move left bound
I'm praising Him in the dance
When I tap on my chest as if I'm signaling my heart
I know what I'm doing
I'm praising Him in the spirit
When I am playing my string instrument and my head turns
left and right
Nothin' wrong sister
I'm just praising Him in the spirit
When my hands are raised in style
Performing a duty so worthwhile
I'm praising Him for His goodness
When my body shakes in a particular form
As my gratitude intensity rises to transform
Don't mind me
I'm just praising Him
When my right leg makes that move that Satan understands
not
And my left leg boogies with a move of "thanks a lot"
Nothin' wrong brother
It's just a praise thing
A wrist or finger may glitter in appreciation
When my hand moves in a thankful motion
It's no show off y'all
I'm only fulfilling an obligation
My eyes are closed as I'm praying,
Unreservedly and intensively thanking
For His goodness, over His caring,
Never you worry
I'm just connecting to Chineke.

Want to Love But Don't Know How

I met them but still don't know how
They wave and fake a smile
They lift you up in your presence
Then burn you in your absence

They even exalt you while you're there
They grin and sometimes counterfeit a laugh
They sometimes praise you while you're there
Then rip you once you're gone

Drawn by everything you do
Nosy and thinks like a devil
They want to see you out
Even when they don't want what you've got.

Though fresh pain unveiled a forgiven day
Still my faith is the unwavering substance of my hope
Forgive those that know not how
For they want to love but don't know how.

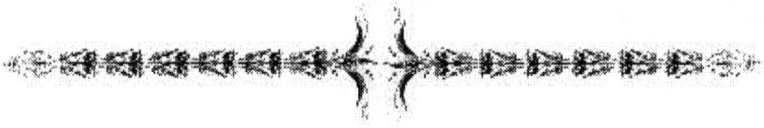

Family

Hold my hands
Walk with me through
These fields of positive expectation
Pray as I pray
Plow as I plow
Release your lights as I release
Let's quench darkness and glow
Illuminate, elucidate and light up
Release your greatness
Shed light on those dark corners
Sow the best seeds
Water as I water
Our God will make our seeds
Bring forth much fruit
I see a future that's gracious
God's children praising a lot
And not asking a lot
Relationship with humans improves daily
Our rapport with God blooms and blossoms
Get closer and you'll see a full cup
I see a tomorrow that's more prosperous
We are ever blessed
We will remain blessed
Hold my hands tight
Squeeze if you care
Walk with me through
These fields of hope, I beseech
And focus with me to this point
From which love showers seem to proceed.

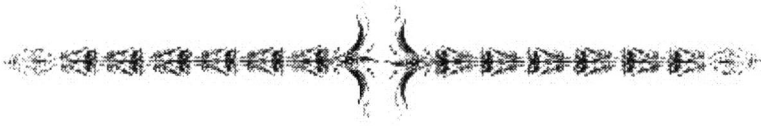

Real Worship

Sometimes have I wondered if this
Lifestyle of mine is totally acceptable
Unto you lord as worship
For when all components of my worship get so right
Uncertainty undoubtedly disappears
The dust of ambiguity clears up
And my spiritual vision celebrates
The dawn of greatness
The curtain of my recognition opens
And ushers in the breezes of love
It always feels like the morning of hope
A new term of pure expectations
Like a new season stuffed in excellence
My worship draws the attention of
Grace and greatness
Your real worship draws too
We have the same God
Jehovah Jireh--- our Provider
Jehovah Rapha—our healer
Jehovah Raah ---- our shepherd
We worship Him the same way
Though your ways may ring better in your ear
But we worship Him in truth and in spirit
As we clear up the dust of uncertainty
And nothing else matters.

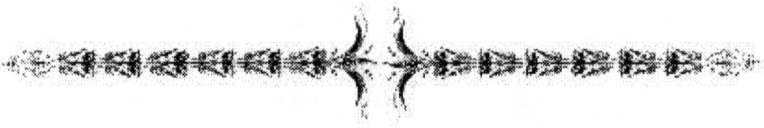

We Worship a Living God

Accept our songs of worship lord
Anoint our tongue suitably
True songs of worship will continually be in our mouth
Unto you father
We lift up our hands in humble awe
Unto you Jehovah Tsidkenu
The lord our righteousness
We totally surrender in meek mode
Unto you Jehovah Shammah
The lord my peace
We give all our worship
Never let the enemy acquire any part of our lives
Today
We exalt thee
Yesterday
We exalted thee
Tomorrow
We will exalt thee
Unto you Jehovah nissi
The lord our banner
Do we sing these songs of worship in total adoration
Never let the enemy get the last laugh
Take total adulation
Take total honor
Take total admiration
Never let the enemy question the authenticity of our God.

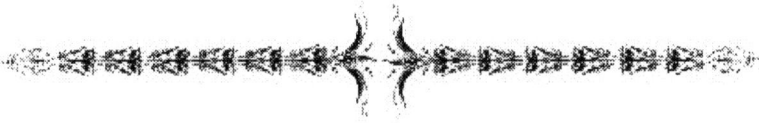

Come Let's Praise Him

In a leg-edez Benz
Let's praise Him
In a Ford Granada
Let's praise Him
On a motorcycle
Let's praise Him
On a bicycle
Let's praise Him
In a Mercedes Benz
Let's praise Him in every situation and location

When God's favor drowns you
Let's praise Him
When the gift is on the way
Let's praise Him
In the offices A & B
Let's praise Him
In the bedroom
Let's praise Him
In the church
Let's praise for in His holy embrace do we come home to
perch

For protection
We'll praise Him
For kindness
We'll praise Him
For direction
We'll praise Him
For Healing
We'll praise Him
For rebuking the devourer
We'll praise Him in the firmament of His Power

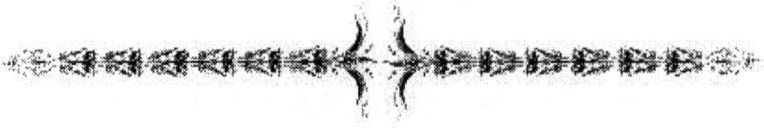

It Will Rain

I know it will rain heavily
These grateful tears of the saints
Have activated the overflow gates of heaven
Our container will be full and spilling over

We receive these showers of prosperity
Our souls cry out in joy
We know that it will rain heavily
Our prayers have triggered a heavy downpour

Let it rain on our soul
It will rain on our health
Let it rain on our bank accounts
Heavy rain of prosperity for the chosen.

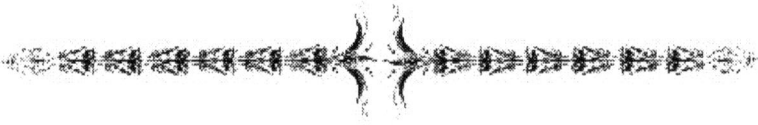

Sacrifices of Gratitude

Lord, we offer you these sacrifices of gratitude;
The urge is real and overly justified.
Your love has sealed these broken hearts together;
In plain English will these hearts express thanks
Knowing so well that
An explicit appreciation enhances a steady flow.

For the thing's you've done for us Lord
We thank you
For the things you are doing right now Lord
We thank you
For the things you are about to do Lord
We thank you

For being our great provider Lord
We thank You
For being our Solid Rock, Rock
We thank You
For building a fence around us Lord
We thank You

For making a way where there's no way Lord
We thank You
For doing us the way you do us Lord
We thank You
For being a light unto our path Lord
We thank You

Sacrifices of praise have become my obligation
So meaningless has some other sacrifices become today
God's love has sealed a broken heart together
And I know so well that
My Plain gratitude will uphold a constant supply.

About the Author

Dr. Udo F. Ufomadu, Ph.D., is the Manager & Publisher of Ufomadu Consulting & Publishing (UC&P), a business consulting/publishing firm based in Selma, Alabama. The firm specializes in business planning and book publishing. He is the author of the highly acclaimed books:

♦ *Anthology of Inspiration*

♦ *How to Become Extremely Successful in Business Management, Personal Management, and Family Budget Planning*

♦ *Quote the Best Out of You*

Dr. Ufomadu has 14 years of experience as a Consumer Food Safety Protection Specialist working with business management in regulatory and inspection capacity for the state of Alabama. He inspects, reviews, monitors, and verifies a food industry's procedures in HACCP/SSOP plans.

He is trained and certified in handling diversity in the work place. He earned a Ph.D. in Business Administration from Madison University, a Master of Science in Administration and Supervision from Alabama State University, additional Master courses in Personnel Management from Troy State, and a Bachelor of Science in Business Administration/Management from Troy State

University. He also attended the College of the Redwoods.

Dr. Udo Ufomadu was inducted as a member of the Institute of Management Consultants (IMC) in 2002. He is a professional member of American Management Association (AMA) and a professional member of the Institute of Food Technologists (IFT), and a professional member of the International Association of Conflict Management. He is also a member of Tabernacle of Praise Church in Selma.

Dr. Ufomadu, also a 2003 and a 2004 Editor's Choice Award (International Library of Poetry) winning inspirational poet, consults nationally and internationally. He is married with four children.

To order additional copies of:

Secrets of Elevation

Hidden in

Stirring Poems

Call 334-418-0088
Or please visit our website at:
www.UfomaduConsulting.com